★★★★★★ AMERICA COOKS ★★★★★★
southern favorites

★★★★★★ AMERICA COOKS ★★★★★★★

southern favorites

mouthwatering meals from Dixie, the Delta, and down on the Bayou

lindley boegehold

southwater

This edition is published by Southwater

Southwater is an imprint of Anness Publishing Ltd, Hermes House, 88–89 Blackfriars Road, London SE1 8HA
tel. 020 7401 2077; fax 020 7633 9499 www.southwaterbooks.com; info@anness.com

© Anness Publishing Ltd 1995, 2002

Published in the USA by Southwater
Anness Publishing Inc
fax 212 807 6813

Distributed in the UK by The Manning Partnership
tel. 01225 852 727; fax 01225 852 852
sales@manning-partnership.co.uk

Distributed in the USA by National Book Network
tel. 301 459 3366; fax 301 459 1705
www.nbnbooks.com

Distributed in Canada by General Publishing
tel. 416 445 3333; fax 416 445 5991
www.genpub.com

Distributed in Australia by Sandstone Publishing
tel. 02 9560 7888; fax 02 9560 7488
sales@sandstonepublishing.com.au

Distributed in New Zealand by
The Five Mile Press (NZ) Ltd
tel. (09) 444 4144; fax (09) 444 4518; fivemilenz@clear.net.nz

All rights reserved. No part of this publication may be reproduced, stored in a retrieval system,
or transmitted in any way or by any means, electronic, mechanical, photocopying, recording or otherwise,
without the prior written permission of the copyright holder.

A CIP catalogue record for this book is available from the British Library.

Publisher: Joanna Lorenz
Managing Editor: Helen Sudell
Designer: Nigel Partridge
Photographer: Amanda Haywood and Robert Harding (p 6/7)
Illustrations by: Estelle Corke
Recipes by: Carla Capalbo and Laura Washburn

Front cover shows a variation of Seafood and Sausage Gumbo – for recipe, see p 30

Previously published as *Southern Family Favorites*

1 3 5 7 9 10 8 6 4 2

NOTES

Standard spoon and cup measures are level.
Large eggs are used unless otherwise stated.

Contents

SOUPS AND STARTERS 8

MAIN COURSES 18

LIGHT SNACKS AND ACCOMPANIMENTS 42

DESSERTS 50

INDEX 64

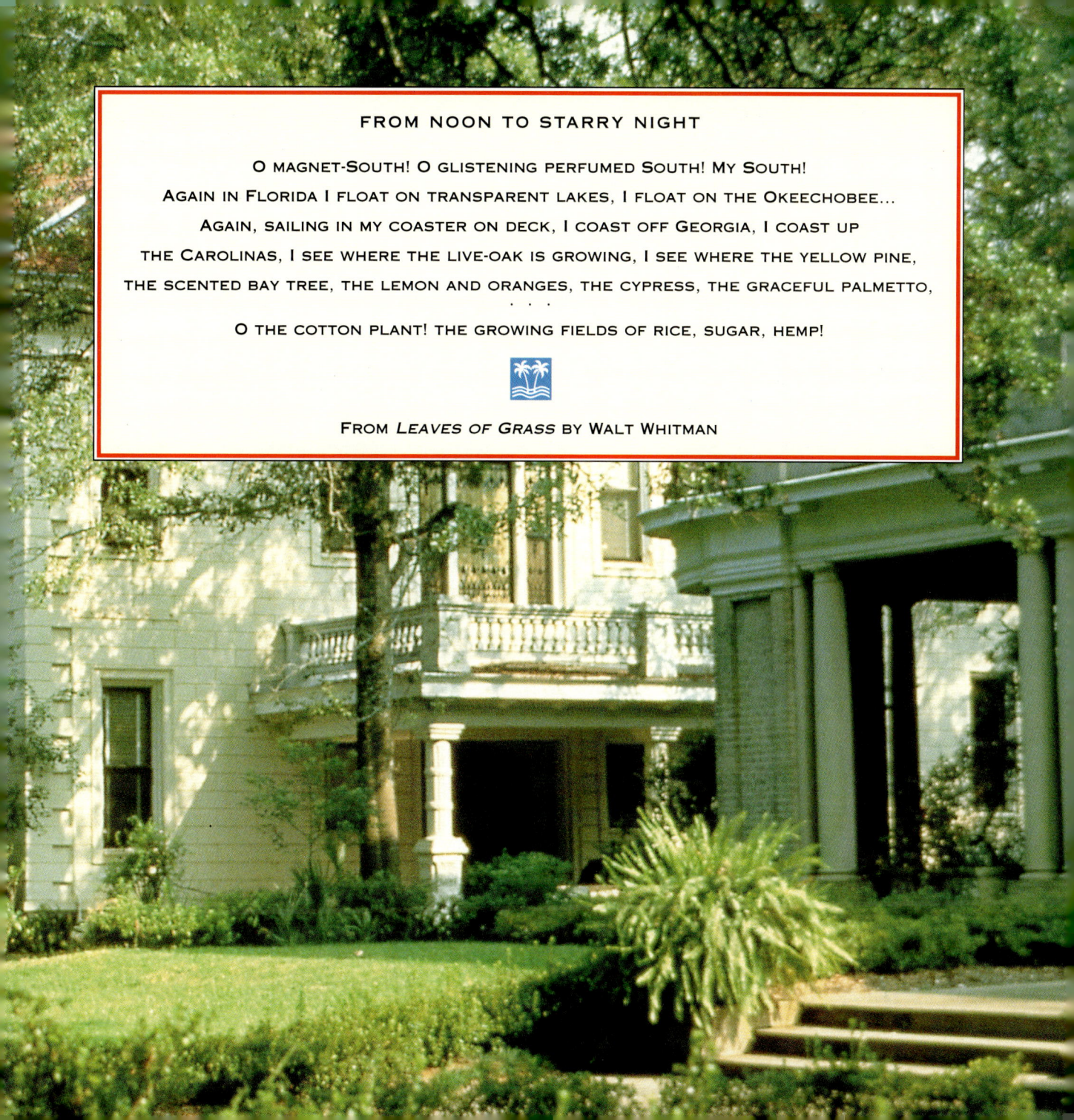

FROM NOON TO STARRY NIGHT

O magnet-South! O glistening perfumed South! My South!
Again in Florida I float on transparent lakes, I float on the Okeechobee...
Again, sailing in my coaster on deck, I coast off Georgia, I coast up
the Carolinas, I see where the live-oak is growing, I see where the yellow pine,
the scented bay tree, the lemon and oranges, the cypress, the graceful palmetto,
. . .
O the cotton plant! the growing fields of rice, sugar, hemp!

From *Leaves of Grass* by Walt Whitman

SOUPS AND STARTERS

MIAMI CHILLED AVOCADO SOUP

If possible use Hass avocados for this creamy, tangy soup. They have bumpy, blackish skins and are richer and tastier than the bigger, green, smooth-skinned variety.

SERVES 4

2 large or 3 medium-size ripe avocados
1 tablespoon fresh lemon juice
¾ cup coarsely chopped peeled cucumber
2 tablespoons dry sherry wine
¼ cup coarsely chopped scallions, with some of the green stems
2 cups mild-flavored chicken stock
1 teaspoon salt
hot pepper sauce (optional)
plain yogurt or cream, for serving

Halve the avocados, remove the pits, and peel. Roughly chop the flesh and place in a food processor or blender. Add the lemon juice, and process until very smooth.

Add the cucumber, sherry wine, and most of the scallions. Process again until smooth.

In a large bowl, combine the avocado mix with the chicken stock. Whisk until well blended. Season with the salt and a few drops of hot pepper sauce, if desired. Cover and chill well.

To serve, fill individual bowls with the soup. Place a spoonful of yogurt or cream in the center of each bowl and swirl with a spoon (see above). Sprinkle with the reserved scallions.

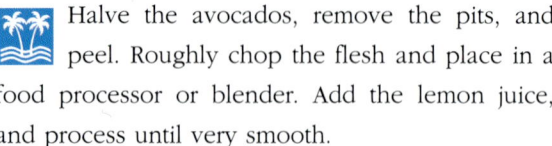

SOUPS AND STARTERS

SHRIMP AND CORN BISQUE

Float a couple of pink shrimp on each serving of this delicious golden soup. Shrimp and corn are a classic Southern combination.

SERVES 4

2 tablespoons olive oil
1 onion, minced
4 tablespoons butter or margarine
¼ cup flour
3 cups fish or chicken stock, or clam juice
1 cup milk
1 cup peeled cooked small shrimp, deveined if necessary
1½ cups corn kernels (fresh, frozen, or canned)
½ teaspoon minced fresh dill or thyme
salt
hot pepper sauce
½ cup light cream

Heat the olive oil in a large heavy saucepan. Add the onion and cook over low heat until softened, about 8-10 minutes.

Meanwhile, melt the butter or margarine in a medium-size saucepan. Add the flour and stir with a wire whisk until blended. Cook 1-2 minutes. Pour in the stock and milk and stir to blend. Bring to a boil over medium heat and cook about 5-8 minutes, stirring frequently.

Cut each shrimp into 2 or 3 pieces and add to the onion with the corn and dill or thyme (see below). Cook for approximately 2-3 minutes, stirring occasionally. Remove the pan from the heat.

Add the sauce mixture to the shrimp and corn mixture and mix together well. Remove 3 cups of the soup and purée in a food processor or blender. Return this mixture to the rest of the soup in the pan and stir well.

Season with salt and hot pepper sauce to taste.

Add the cream and stir to blend. Heat the soup almost to boiling point, stirring frequently.

Serve while still piping hot.

SOUPS AND STARTERS

PALM BEACH PAPAYA AND AVOCADO SALAD

THIS PERFECT SUMMER LUNCHEON DISH IS AS LUXURIOUS AND RICH AS ITS NAME. IT CALLS UP GREEN LAWNS, TALL ICED DRINKS AND ENDLESS BALMY AFTERNOONS.

SERVES 4

2 ripe avocados
1 ripe papaya
1 large sweet orange
1 small red onion
2 cups small arugula leaves, washed and spun dry

FOR THE DRESSING

¼ cup olive oil
2 tablespoons fresh lemon or lime juice
salt and pepper

Halve the avocados and remove the pits. Carefully peel off the skin. Cut each avocado half lengthwise into 4 thick slices.

With a sharp knife, peel the papaya. Cut it lengthwise and scoop out the seeds with a spoon (see below left). Set aside 1 teaspoon of the seeds for the dressing. Cut each papaya half lengthwise into 8 slices.

Peel the orange. Using a sharp paring knife, cut out the sections, cutting on either side of the dividing membranes. Cut the onion into very thin slices and separate into rings.

Combine the dressing ingredients in a bowl and mix well. Stir in the reserved papaya seeds.

Assemble the salad on 4 individual serving plates. Alternate slices of papaya and avocado and add the orange sections and a small mound of arugula topped with onion rings. Spoon on the dressing and serve.

COOK'S TIP

AS AVOCADO DOES NOT KEEP AT ALL WELL, A LITTLE LEMON JUICE SQUEEZED ONTO THE FLESH WILL STOP IT FROM DISCOLORING FOR A FEW HOURS.

SOUPS AND STARTERS

Warm Salad of Black-eyed Peas

In the South, eating black-eyed peas is a New Year's Day tradition that brings good luck in the coming year. This jazzed-up warm salad tastes good all year round.

Serves 4

2 small red bell peppers
½ teaspoon Dijon-style mustard
2 tablespoons wine vinegar
¼ teaspoon salt
⅛ teaspoon pepper
6 tablespoons olive oil
2 tablespoons minced fresh chives
3 cups fresh black-eyed peas
1 bay leaf
8 lean bacon slices

Preheat the broiler.

Broil the bell peppers until the skin blackens and blisters, turning the peppers so that all sides are charred (see right). Remove from the broiler and place the peppers in a paper or plastic bag to steam. Let cool 10 minutes.

Peel off the skin. Cut the peppers in half, discard the seeds, white membranes, and stem, and slice into ½- x 2-inch strips. Set aside.

Combine the mustard and vinegar in a small bowl. Add the salt and pepper. Beat in the oil until well blended. Add the chives.

Add the black-eyed peas to a pan of boiling salted water, with the bay leaf. Boil until just tender, 13-15 minutes.

Meanwhile, cook the bacon until crisp. Drain on paper towels. Cut or break into small pieces.

When the peas are done, drain them and discard the bay leaf. Toss them with the chive dressing.

Make a mound of peas on a serving dish. Sprinkle with the bacon pieces and garnish with the strips of red pepper. Serve warm.

COOK'S TIP

If preferred, chop the roasted red peppers rather than cutting them into strips and mix into the warm black-eyed peas.

SOUPS AND STARTERS

FROMAJARDIS

These bite-sized cheese-filled canapes are perfect party food because they can be made ahead of time. Let them cool on a wire rack then store in an airtight container. Just before the guests arrive reheat them in a preheated 375°F oven for 5-10 minutes.

MAKES ABOUT 40

2 cups flour
¼ teaspoon grated nutmeg
½ teaspoon salt
10 tablespoons cold butter or shortening, or a combination of both
6-8 tablespoons ice water

FOR THE FILLING

2 eggs
¼ pound sharp cheddar cheese, shredded (about 1 cup)
hot pepper sauce
1 tablespoon minced mixed fresh herbs, such as thyme, chives, and sage

For the pastry, sift the flour, nutmeg, and salt into a bowl. Using a pastry blender or 2 knives, cut the butter or shortening into the dry ingredients as quickly as possible until the mixture is crumbly and resembles coarse meal.

Sprinkle 6 tablespoons of the ice water over the flour mixture. Combine with a fork until the dough holds together. If the dough is too crumbly, add a little more water. Gather the dough into a ball.

Divide the dough in half and pat each portion into a disk. Wrap the disks in wax paper and refrigerate them at least 20 minutes.

Preheat the oven to 425°F.

For the filling, put the eggs in a mixing bowl and beat well with a fork. Add the cheese, hot pepper sauce to taste, and the herbs.

On a lightly floured surface, roll out the dough to a thickness of ⅛-inch or less. Cut out rounds using a 3-inch cookie cutter or drinking glass.

Place 1 teaspoon of filling in the center of each pastry round. Fold over to make half-moon shapes, and press the edges together with the tines of a fork. A bit of filling may ooze through the seam.

Cut a few small slashes in the top of each pastry with the point of a sharp knife. Place on ungreased baking sheets. Bake until the pastries start to darken slightly, 18-20 minutes. The pastry should be cooked through when cut in half. Serve warm.

COOK'S TIP

The fromajardis may be made ahead of time. Let them cool on a wire rack and then store in an airtight container. Reheat before serving.

MAIN COURSES

CRAB BAYOU

This dish takes its name from the sea marshes and swamps of Louisiana that teem with all kinds of shellfish. Both Cajun and Creole cuisines have devised simple yet elegant dishes to celebrate this bounty.

SERVES 6

1 pound fresh lump crab meat
3 hard-cooked egg yolks
1 teaspoon Dijon-style mustard
6 tablespoons butter or margarine, at room temperature
¼ teaspoon cayenne
3 tablespoons sherry wine
2 tablespoons minced fresh parsley
½ cup whipping cream
½ cup thinly sliced scallions, including some of the green stems
salt and black pepper
½ cup dry bread crumbs

Preheat the oven to 350°F.

Pick over the crab meat and remove any shell or cartilage, keeping the pieces of crab as big as possible (see below left).

In a medium-size bowl, crumble the egg yolks with a fork. Add the mustard, 4 tablespoons of the butter or margarine, and the cayenne, and mash together to form a paste.

Mash in the sherry wine and parsley.

Mix the cream and scallions. Stir in the crab meat. Season with salt and pepper.

Divide the mixture equally among 6 greased scallop shells (other individual baking dishes will do if you do not have scallop shells).

Sprinkle with the bread crumbs and dot with the remaining butter or margarine.

Bake until bubbling hot and golden brown, about 20 minutes.

Serve immediately.

MAIN COURSES

Cajun "Popcorn" with Basil mayonnaise

So-called because they are as light and addictive as popcorn and are served in bowls at bars and restaurants down on the bayou.

Serves 8

2 pounds raw crawfish tails, peeled, or small shrimp, peeled and deveined
2 eggs
1 cup dry white wine
½ cup fine cornmeal (or all-purpose flour, if not available)
½ cup all-purpose flour
1 tablespoon minced fresh chives
1 garlic clove, minced
½ teaspoon fresh thyme leaves
¼ teaspoon salt
¼ teaspoon cayenne
¼ teaspoon black pepper
oil for deep-frying

For the mayonnaise

1 egg yolk
2 teaspoons Dijon-style mustard
1 tablespoon white wine vinegar
salt and pepper
1 cup olive or vegetable oil
½ cup minced fresh basil leaves

Rinse the crawfish tails or shrimp in cool running water. Drain well on paper towels and set aside in a cool place.

Mix together the eggs and wine in a small bowl.

In a mixing bowl, combine the cornmeal and/or flour, chives, garlic, thyme, salt, cayenne, and pepper. Gradually whisk in the egg mixture, blending well. Cover the batter and let stand 1 hour at room temperature.

For the mayonnaise, combine the egg yolk, mustard, and vinegar in a mixing bowl. Add salt and pepper to taste. Add the oil in a thin stream, beating vigorously with a wire whisk. When the mixture is thick and smooth, stir in the minced basil. Cover and refrigerate until you are ready to serve.

Heat 2-3 inches of oil in a large skillet or deep-fryer to 365-370°F. Dip the seafood into the batter and fry until golden brown, 2-3 minutes. It is best to fry the seafood in small batches. Turn as necessary for even coloring. Remove with a slotted spoon and drain on paper towels. Serve hot, with the basil mayonnaise.

MAIN COURSES

Crawfish or Shrimp Etouffée

When making Cajun roux take great care not to burn the flour. If it does burn, throw it away and start again or the dish will have a bitter burned taste.

Serves 6

2½ pounds raw crawfish or shrimp in shell, with heads
3 cups water
⅓ cup vegetable oil or lard
⅓ cup flour
¾ cup minced onions
¼ cup minced green bell peppers
¼ cup minced celery
1 garlic clove, minced
½ cup dry white wine
2 tablespoons butter or margarine
½ cup minced fresh parsley
¼ cup minced fresh chives
salt
hot pepper sauce
rice, for serving

Peel and devein the crawfish or shrimp; reserve the heads and shells. Keep the seafood in a covered bowl in the refrigerator.

Put the heads and shells in a large pot with the water. Bring to a boil, cover, and simmer 15 minutes. Strain and reserve 1½ cups of stock. Set aside.

To make the Cajun roux, heat the oil or lard in a heavy castiron skillet. (Do not use a nonstick pan.)

When the oil is hot, add the flour, a little at a time, and blend to a smooth paste using a long-handled flat-bottomed wooden spoon.

Cook over medium-low heat, stirring constantly, until the Cajun roux reaches the desired color, 25-40 minutes. It will gradually deepen in color from light beige to tan, to a deeper, redder brown. When it reaches the color of peanut butter, remove the pan from the heat and immediately mix in the onions, bell pepper, and celery. Continue stirring to prevent further darkening.

Return the pan to low heat. Add the garlic and cook 1-2 minutes, stirring. Add the seafood stock and blend well with a wire whisk. Whisk in the white wine.

Bring to a boil, stirring, and simmer until the sauce is thick, 3-4 minutes. Remove from the heat.

In a large heavy saucepan, melt the butter or margarine. Add the crawfish or shrimp, stir, and cook until pink, 2-3 minutes. Stir in the herbs.

Add the sauce and stir well to combine. Season with salt and hot pepper sauce to taste. Simmer over medium heat 3-4 minutes. Serve hot with rice.

MAIN COURSES

SHRIMP CREOLE

CREOLE CUISINE ORIGINATED IN NEW ORLEANS AND DRAWS FROM MANY ETHNIC CUISINES: FRENCH, SPANISH, ITALIAN, NATIVE AMERICAN AND AFRICAN. THIS CLASSIC CREOLE DISH INCLUDES THE REQUIRED TRIO OF ONIONS, CELERY AND BELL PEPPERS.

SERVES 4

1½ pounds raw shrimp in shell, with heads if available
2 cups water
3 tablespoons olive or vegetable oil
1½ cups minced onions
½ cup minced celery
½ cup minced green bell pepper
½ cup chopped fresh parsley
1 garlic clove, minced
1 tablespoon Worcestershire sauce
¼ teaspoon cayenne
½ cup chopped peeled plum tomatoes
1 teaspoon salt
1 bay leaf
1 teaspoon sugar
rice, for serving

Peel and devein the shrimp; reserve the heads and shells. Keep the shrimp chilled in a covered bowl in the refrigerator while you make the sauce.

Put the shrimp heads and shells in a saucepan with the water. Bring to a boil and simmer 15 minutes. Strain and reserve 1½ cups of this stock. Set the stock aside.

Heat the oil in a heavy saucepan. Add the onions and cook over low heat until softened, 8-10 minutes. Add the celery and bell pepper and cook 5 minutes more. Stir in the parsley, garlic, Worcestershire sauce, and cayenne. Cook another 5 minutes, stirring occasionally.

Raise the heat to medium. Stir in the wine and simmer 3-4 minutes. Add the tomatoes, shrimp stock, salt, bay leaf, and sugar and bring to a boil. Stir well, then reduce the heat to low and simmer until the tomatoes have fallen apart and the sauce has reduced slightly, about 30 minutes. Remove from the heat and let cool slightly.

Remove and discard the bay leaf. Pour the sauce into a food processor or blender and purée until quite smooth. Taste and adjust the seasoning if required.

Return the sauce to the pan and bring to a boil. Add the shrimp and simmer until they turn pink, 4-5 minutes only. Serve immediately with rice.

MAIN COURSES

Shrimp-stuffed Eggplant

—

This sublime dish has Italian roots. It resembles an Eggplant Parmesan with the inspired addition of shrimp.

Serves 4

2 large firm eggplants, of equal size
2 tablespoons fresh lemon juice
3 tablespoons butter or margarine
½ pound raw shrimp, peeled and deveined
½ cup thinly sliced scallions, including some green stems
1½ cups chopped fresh tomatoes
1 garlic clove, minced
¼ cup chopped fresh parsley
¼ cup chopped fresh basil
⅛ teaspoon grated nutmeg
salt and pepper
hot pepper sauce
½ cup dry bread crumbs
rice, for serving

Preheat the oven to 375°F.

Cut the eggplants in half lengthwise. With a small sharp knife, cut around the inside edge of each eggplant half, about ½ inch from the skin. Carefully scoop out the flesh, leaving a shell of about ½ inch thick.

Immerse the shells, skin side up, in cold water to prevent them from discoloring.

Chop the scooped-out eggplant flesh coarsely, toss with the lemon juice, and set aside.

Melt 2 tablespoons of the butter or margarine in a skillet. Add the shrimp and sauté until pink, 2-3 minutes, turning so they cook evenly. Remove the shrimp with a slotted spoon and set aside.

Add the scallions to the skillet and cook over medium heat about 2 minutes, stirring. Add the tomatoes, garlic, and parsley and cook 5 minutes.

Add the chopped eggplant, basil, and nutmeg. If necessary, add a little water to prevent the vegetables sticking. Mix well. Cover and simmer 8-10 minutes. Remove from the heat.

Cut each shrimp into 2 or 3 pieces. Stir into the vegetable mixture. Season with salt, pepper, and hot sauce to taste.

Lightly oil a shallow baking pan large enough to hold the eggplant halves in one layer. Drain and dry the eggplant shells and arrange in the pan.

Sprinkle a layer of bread crumbs into each shell. Spoon in a layer of the shrimp mixture. Repeat, finishing with a layer of crumbs.

Dot with the remaining butter or margarine. Bake until golden brown on top, 20-25 minutes. Serve immediately, accompanied by rice, if desired.

MAIN COURSES

Fried Catfish Fillets with Piquant Sauce

All along the coast from South Carolina to Florida you'll find this quintessentially southern fish dish. Some restaurants pop a bottle of Tabasco sauce on the table; this recipe provides its own homemade sauce.

Serves 4

1 egg
¼ cup olive oil
squeeze of lemon juice
½ teaspoon minced fresh dill or parsley
salt and pepper
4 catfish fillets
½ cup flour
2 tablespoons butter or margarine

For the sauce

1 egg yolk
2 tablespoons Dijon-style mustard
2 tablespoons white wine vinegar
2 teaspoons paprika
1¼ cups olive or vegetable oil
2 tablespoons prepared horseradish
½ teaspoon minced garlic
¼ cup minced celery
2 tablespoons catsup
½ teaspoon pepper
½ teaspoon salt

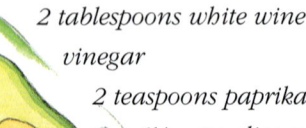

 For the sauce, combine the egg yolk, mustard, vinegar, and paprika in a mixing bowl. Add the oil in a thin stream, beating vigorously with a wire whisk to blend it in.

When the mixture is smooth and thick, beat in all the other sauce ingredients. Cover and refrigerate until ready to serve.

Combine the egg, 1 tablespoon olive oil, the lemon juice, herbs, and a little salt and pepper in a shallow dish. Beat until well combined.

Dip both sides of each catfish fillet in the egg and herb mixture, then coat lightly with flour, shaking off the excess.

Heat the butter or margarine with the remaining olive oil in a large heavy skillet or frying pan. Add the fillets and fry until golden brown on both sides and cooked, 8-10 minutes. To test for doneness, insert the point of a sharp knife into the fish: it should still be opaque in the center.

Serve the catfish fillets hot, with the sauce.

Variation

If preferred, serve the catfish fillets with lime or lemon wedges.

MAIN COURSES

Seafood and Sausage Gumbo

This typical Cajun dish calls for many of the primary ingredients of the cuisine; shrimp, garlic, okra, cayenne and andouille sausage. Be sure to use a heavy-bottomed, preferably cast-iron skillet; the roux won't brown properly in a nonstick pan.

Serves 10-12

3 pounds raw shrimp in shell
7 cups water
1 onion, quartered
4 bay leaves
¾ cup vegetable oil
1 cup flour
4 tablespoons margarine or butter
3 cups minced onions
2 cups minced green bell pepper
2 cups minced celery
1½ pounds kielbasa (Polish) or andouille sausage, cut in ½-inch rounds
1 pound fresh okra, cut in ½-inch slices
3 garlic cloves
½ teaspoon fresh or dried thyme leaves
2 teaspoons salt
½ teaspoon black pepper
½ teaspoon white pepper
1 teaspoon cayenne
hot pepper sauce (optional)
2 cups chopped peeled fresh or canned plum tomatoes
1 pound fresh lump crab meat
rice, for serving

Peel and devein the shrimp; reserve the heads and shells. Keep the shrimp in a covered bowl in the refrigerator while you make the sauce.

Put the shrimp heads and shells in a saucepan with the water, quartered onion, and 1 bay leaf. Bring to a boil, then partly cover and simmer 20 minutes. Strain and set aside.

MAIN COURSES

Heat the oil in a heavy castiron or steel pan. (Do not use a nonstick pan.) When the oil is hot, add the flour, a little at a time, and gradually blend to a smooth paste using a long-handled flat-bottomed wooden spoon.

Cook over medium-low heat, stirring constantly, until the Cajun roux reaches the desired color, 25-40 minutes. The roux will gradually deepen in color from light beige to tan, to a deeper, redder brown. When it reaches the color of peanut butter, remove the pan from the heat and continue stirring until the roux has cooled and stopped cooking.

Melt the margarine or butter in a large heavy saucepan or Dutch oven. Add the minced onions, bell pepper, and celery. Cook over medium-low heat until the onions are softened, 6-8 minutes, stirring occasionally.

Add the sausage and mix well (see right). Cook 5 minutes. Add the okra and garlic, stir, and cook until the okra stops producing white "threads."

Add the remaining bay leaves, the thyme, salt, black and white peppers, cayenne, and hot pepper sauce to taste, if desired. Mix well. Stir in 6 cups of the shrimp stock and the tomatoes. Bring to a boil, then partly cover the pan, lower the heat, and simmer about 20 minutes.

Whisk in the Cajun roux. Raise the heat and bring to a boil, whisking well. Lower the heat again and simmer, uncovered, 40-50 minutes more, stirring occasionally.

Gently stir in the shrimp and crab meat. Cook until the shrimp turn pink, 3-4 minutes. To serve, put a mound of hot rice in each serving bowl and ladle on the gumbo, making sure each person gets some seafood and some sausage.

COOK'S TIP

HEAVY PANS RETAIN THEIR HEAT. WHEN MAKING A CAJUN ROUX, DO NOT LET IT GET TOO DARK, AS THE ROUX WILL CONTINUE COOKING OFF THE HEAT.

MAIN COURSES

SMOTHERED RABBIT

Arcadian settlers made good use of all the fish and game available in the Louisiana swamp lands. This dish works equally well with chicken if rabbit is unavailable.

SERVES 4

6 tablespoons soy sauce

hot pepper sauce

½ teaspoon white pepper

1 teaspoon sweet paprika

1 teaspoon dried basil

2- to 3-pound rabbit, cut in pieces

3 tablespoons peanut or olive oil

¾ cup flour

2 cups finely sliced onions

1 cup dry white wine

1 cup chicken or meat stock

1 teaspoon salt

1 teaspoon minced garlic

½ cup minced fresh parsley

mashed potatoes or rice, for serving

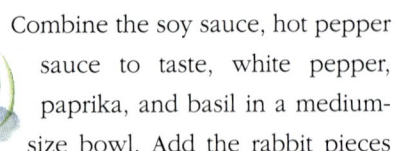

Combine the soy sauce, hot pepper sauce to taste, white pepper, paprika, and basil in a medium-size bowl. Add the rabbit pieces and rub them with the mixture. Let marinate 1 hour.

Heat the oil in a high-sided ovenproof skillet or Dutch oven. Coat the rabbit pieces lightly in the flour, shaking off the excess (see above right).

Brown the rabbit in the hot oil, turning frequently, 5-6 minutes. Remove and set aside.

Preheat the oven to 350°F.

Add the onions to the skillet and cook over low heat until softened, 8-10 minutes. Raise the heat to medium, add the wine, and stir well to mix in all the cooking juices.

Return the rabbit to the skillet. Add the stock, salt, garlic, and parsley. Mix well and turn the rabbit to coat with the sauce.

Cover the skillet and place it in the oven. Cook until the rabbit is tender, about 1 hour, stirring occasionally. Serve with mashed potatoes or rice.

MAIN COURSES

Pork Jambalaya

This hearty stew is an ideal party dish. As the song by the same name instructs: "Fill fruit jar, play guitar and be gay O, Son of a gun we'll have big fun on the bayou."

Serves 6

2½ pounds boneless pork shoulder butt
¼ cup peanut or olive oil
1½ cups minced onions
1 cup minced celery
1½ cups minced green or red bell peppers
1½ cups tasso or other smoked ham, cut in ½-inch cubes
1 teaspoon black pepper
1 teaspoon white pepper
½ teaspoon cayenne
1 teaspoon salt
1 garlic clove, minced
1½ cups chopped peeled fresh or canned tomatoes
1 bay leaf
½ teaspoon fresh or dried thyme leaves
hot pepper sauce
1 cup dry white wine
1 cups long-grain rice
3-4 cups chicken stock, heated

 Remove any visible fat or gristle from the pork, and cut the meat into ½-inch cubes.

Heat the oil in a large pot or Dutch oven. Brown the cubes of pork, in batches, stirring so that it colors evenly. Remove the pork with a slotted spoon and set aside.

Add the onions, celery, and bell peppers to the pot and cook, stirring, 3-4 minutes. Add the ham, black and white peppers, cayenne, and salt. Cook over medium heat, stirring frequently, until the onions are soft and golden, about 12 minutes.

Add the garlic, tomatoes, herbs, and hot pepper sauce to taste. Cook 5 minutes more. Add the pork and wine and mix well, then cover the pot and cook gently over low heat for about 45 minutes.

Add the rice and stir well. Cook 3-4 minutes.

Pour in 3 cups of the chicken stock and stir to blend. Bring to a boil. Cover, reduce the heat to low, and simmer until the rice is tender, about 15 minutes. Stir the mixture occasionally and add more chicken stock if necessary. The rice should be moist, not dry and fluffy.

Serve from the casserole or in a large heated serving dish into large bowls. No accompaniment is needed for this hearty dish.

MAIN COURSES

Pecan-stuffed Pork Chops

Pecans are an essential part of Southern cuisine. In Louisiana they use them to make pralines, in Georgia they go into just about everything. Here they blend their rich taste with pork chops.

Serves 4

4 pork chops, at least 1 inch thick, trimmed of almost all fat
½ cup fresh bread crumbs
½ cup minced scallions
½ cup minced apple
½ cup chopped pecans
1 garlic clove, minced
¼ cup minced fresh parsley
¼ teaspoon cayenne
¼ teaspoon black pepper
½ teaspoon dry mustard
⅛ teaspoon ground cumin
2 tablespoons olive oil
½ cup meat or chicken stock
½ cup dry white wine
1 bay leaf

Preheat the oven to 350°F. Make a pocket in each chop by cutting horizontally from the fatty side straight to the bone.

Combine all the other ingredients except the stock, wine, and bay leaf. Mix well. Divide the mixture among the chops, filling each pocket with as much of the stuffing as it will hold (see above).

Place the chops in a greased baking dish large enough to hold them in one layer.

Pour the stock and wine over them and add the bay leaf and any leftover stuffing. Cover tightly. Bake until tender, about 1 hour, basting occasionally with pan juices. Serve with cooking juices spooned over.

Cook's Tip

Pecan shells are extremely hard to open so always buy pre-shelled nuts.

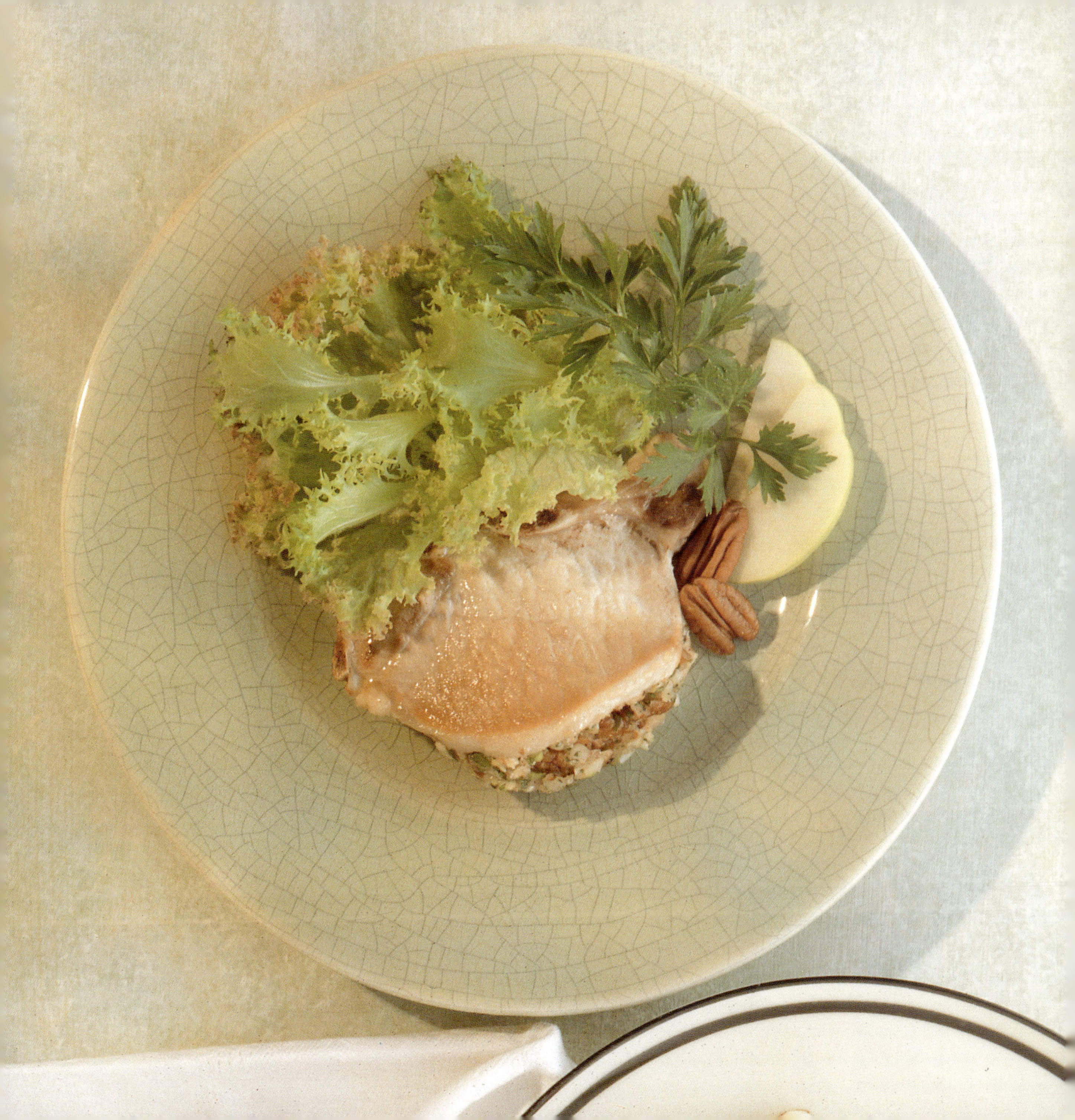

MAIN COURSES

OVEN "FRIED" CHICKEN

This method of baking chicken pieces after they have been dipped in their batter results in an equally crunchy dish that is much lower in fat than the traditional frying technique.

SERVES 4

4 large chicken pieces
½ cup flour
½ teaspoon salt
¼ teaspoon pepper
1 egg
2 tablespoons water
2 tablespoons minced mixed fresh herbs, such as parsley, basil, and thyme
1 cup dry bread crumbs
¼ cup freshly grated Parmesan cheese
lemon wedges, for serving.

Preheat the oven to 400°F.

Rinse the chicken pieces in cool water. Pat dry with paper towels.

Combine the flour, salt, and pepper on a plate and stir with a fork to mix. Coat the chicken pieces on both sides with the seasoned flour and shake off the excess.

Sprinkle a little water onto the chicken pieces, and coat again lightly with the seasoned flour.

Beat the egg with the water in a shallow dish. Stir in the herbs. Dip the chicken pieces into the egg mixture, turning to coat them evenly.

Combine the bread crumbs and grated Parmesan cheese on a plate. Roll the chicken in the crumbs, patting with your fingers to help them to adhere.

Place the chicken pieces in a greased shallow pan large enough to hold them in one layer (see above). Bake until thoroughly cooked and golden, 20-30 minutes. To test for doneness, prick with a fork; the juices that run out should be clear, not pink. Serve hot, with lemon wedges.

COOK'S TIP

These chicken pieces are also delicious cold on picnics or at summer parties.

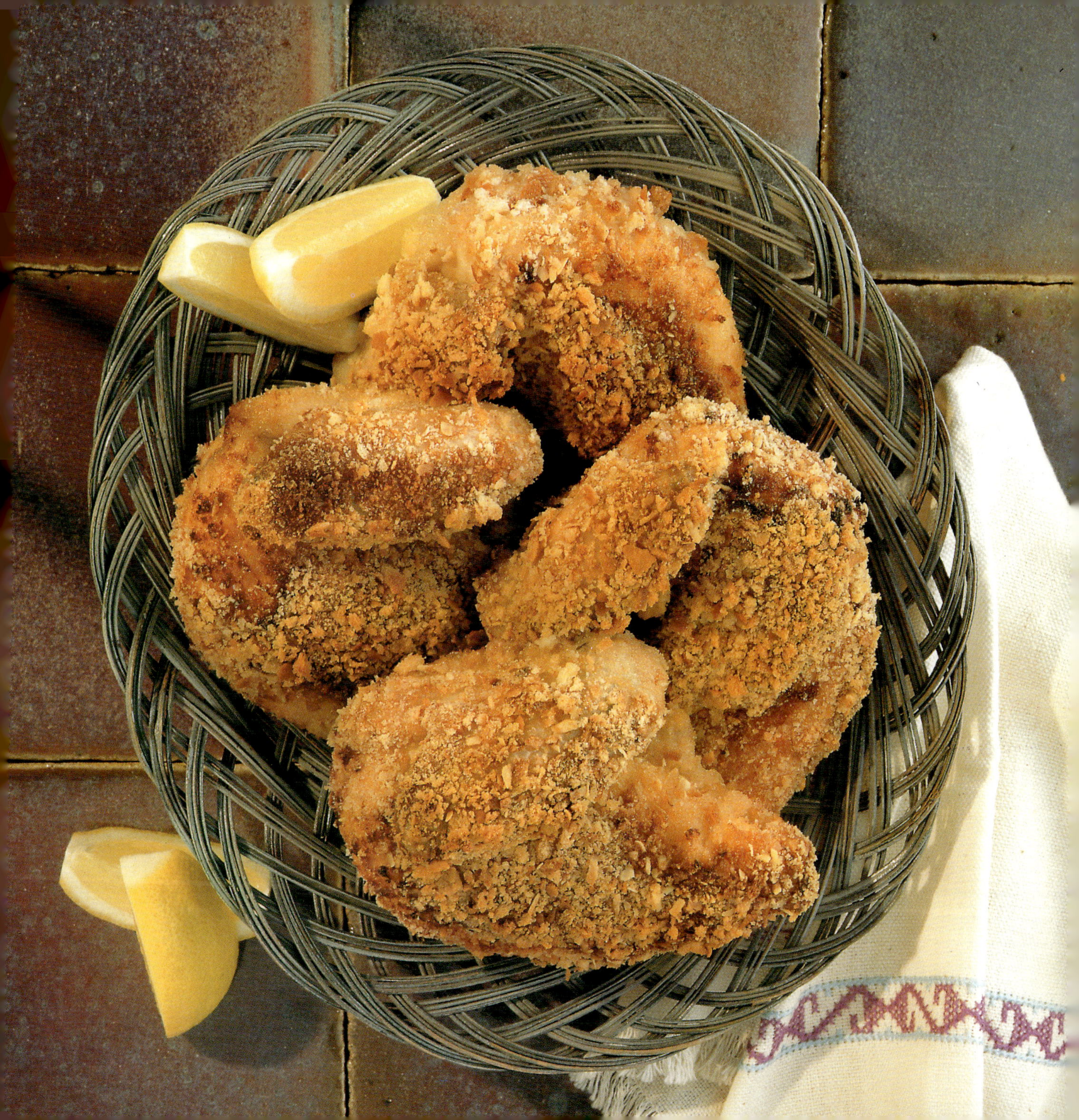

MAIN COURSES

BLACKENED CHICKEN BREASTS

This dramatic technique was invented by Paul Prud'homme, New Orleans chef extraordinaire. He uses fillets of fish, but chicken breasts are also delicious prepared this way.

Serves 6

6 medium-size skinless boneless chicken breast halves

6 tablespoons butter or margarine

1 teaspoon garlic powder

2 teaspoons onion powder

1 teaspoon cayenne

2 teaspoons sweet paprika

1½ teaspoons salt

½ teaspoon white pepper

1 teaspoon black pepper

¼ teaspoon ground cumin

1 teaspoon dried thyme leaves

Slice each chicken breast piece in half horizontally, making 2 pieces of about the same thickness. Flatten slightly with the heel of the hand.

Melt the butter or margarine in a small saucepan.

Combine all the remaining ingredients in a shallow bowl and stir to blend well. Brush the chicken pieces on both sides with melted butter or margarine, then sprinkle evenly with the seasoning mixture.

Heat a large heavy skillet over high heat until a drop of water sprinkled on the surface sizzles. This will take 5-8 minutes.

Drizzle a teaspoon of melted butter on each chicken piece. Place them in the skillet in an even layer, 2 or 3 at a time. Cook until the underside begins to blacken, 2-3 minutes. Turn and cook the other side 2-3 minutes more (see left). Serve hot.

Cook's Tip

To grill the chicken, set on an oiled grill rack 5 inches above the coals, and cook the breasts until lightly charred and cooked through.

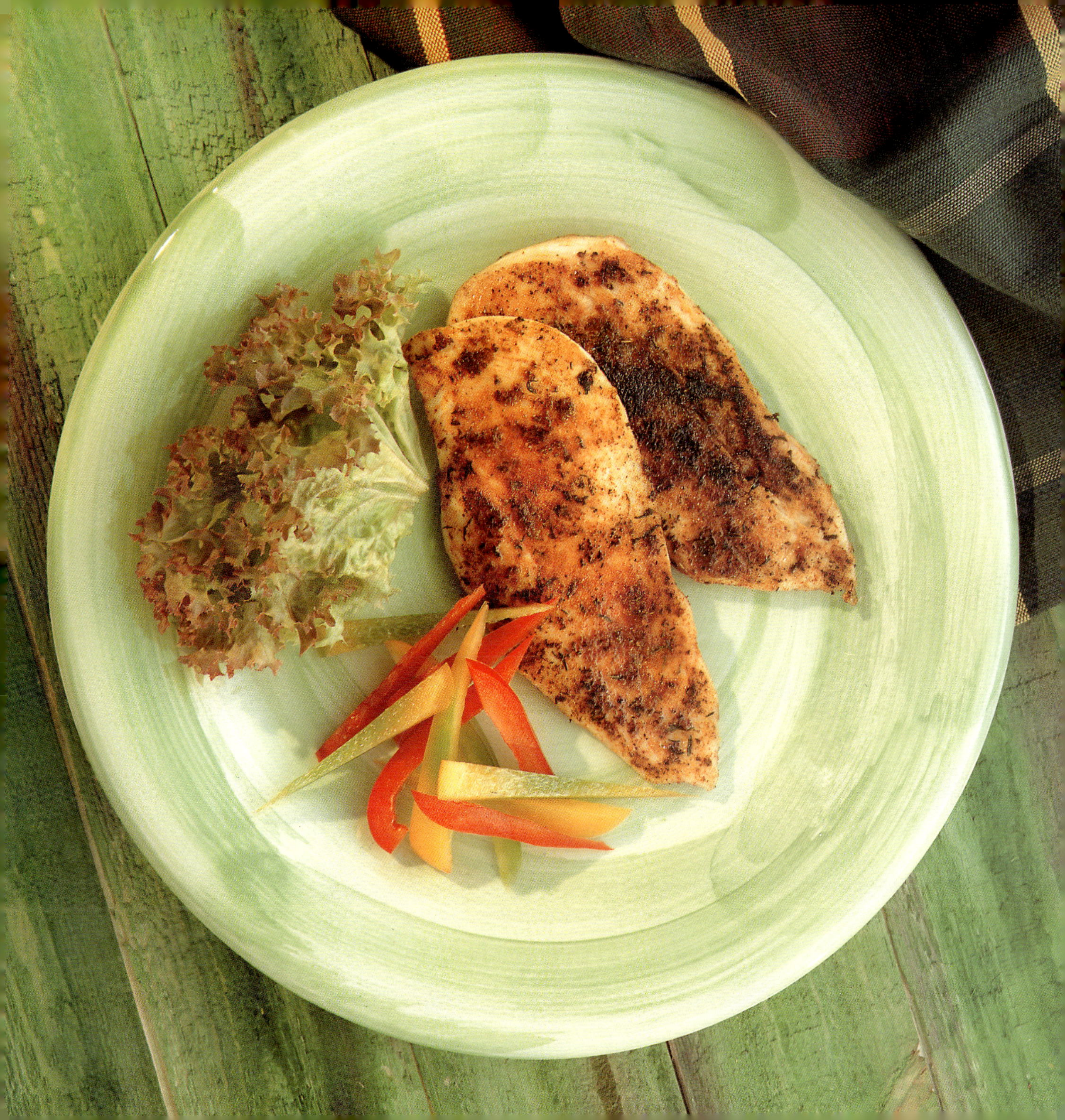

LIGHT SNACKS AND ACCOMPANIMENTS

CORN MAQUE CHOUX

The classic trio of onion, celery and bell pepper make a savory bed for corn kernels.

SERVES 4

2 tablespoons peanut or olive oil
½ cup minced onion
⅓ cup minced celery
⅓ cup minced red bell pepper
3 cups corn kernels (fresh, frozen, or canned)
½ teaspoon cayenne
½ cup dry white wine or water
1 medium tomato, diced
1 teaspoon salt
black pepper
3 tablespoons whipping cream
2 tablespoons shredded fresh basil

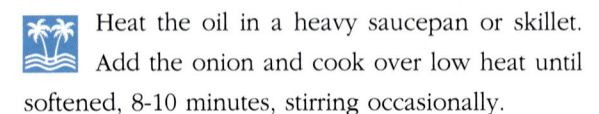

Heat the oil in a heavy saucepan or skillet. Add the onion and cook over low heat until softened, 8-10 minutes, stirring occasionally.

Raise the heat to medium, add the celery and bell pepper, and cook 5 minutes more, stirring.

Stir in the corn kernels and the cayenne and cook until the corn begins to stick to the pan.

Pour in the wine or water and scrape up the corn from the pan. Add the tomato and season. Cook over low heat until the tomato has softened.

Remove from heat, and add the cream and basil.

COLLARDS AND RICE

This side dish is easy to prepare and makes an inexpensive, tasty addition to the table.

SERVES 4

2 cups chicken or meat stock
1 cup long-grain rice
1 tablespoon butter or margarine
½ teaspoon salt
3 cups chopped collard leaves, loosely packed
pepper

Bring the stock to a boil in a medium-size saucepan. Add the rice, butter or margarine, and salt. Stir.

Add the collards, a handful at a time, stirring well after each addition.

Bring back to a boil, then cover, reduce the heat, and cook until the rice is tender, approximately 15-20 minutes.

Season with pepper before serving.

COOK'S TIP

If you can't find collard greens, kale, Swiss chard or spinach can be substituted with equal success. Top with a slice of lemon if desired.

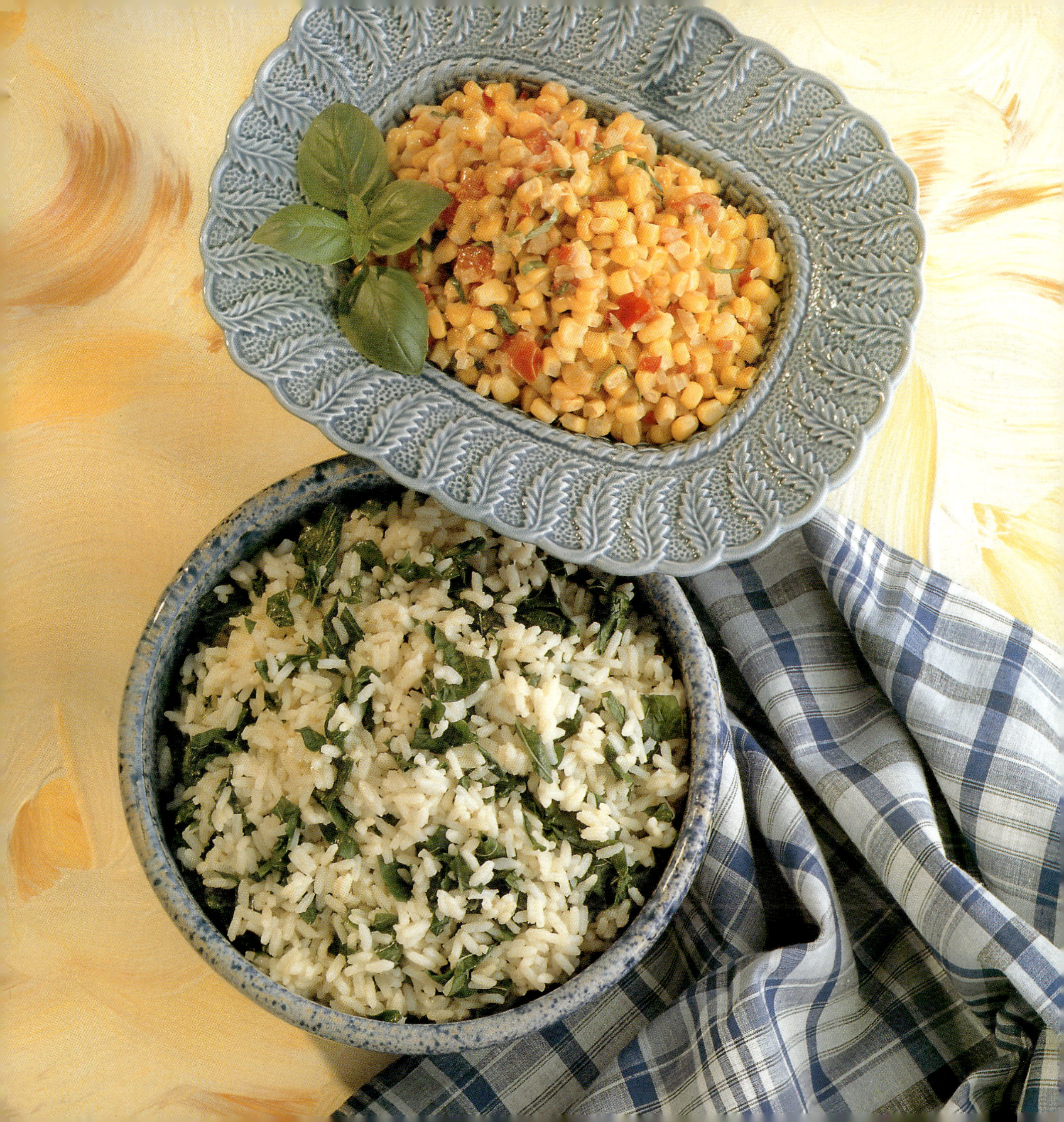

LIGHT SNACKS AND ACCOMPANIMENTS

DIRTY RICE

CHICKEN LIVERS GIVE THIS RICE ITS COLOR AND NAME. SAVOR IT WITH A GLASS OF FULL-BODIED RED WINE.

SERVES 4

6 tablespoons olive or vegetable oil
1 cup minced onion
½ pound ground pork
1 garlic clove, minced
½ pound chicken gizzards, chopped
½ cup minced celery
½ cup minced red or green bell pepper
½ teaspoon white pepper
1 teaspoon cayenne
1 bay leaf
½ teaspoon fresh or dried thyme leaves
1 teaspoon salt
3 cups chicken stock
½ pound chicken livers, chopped
1 cup long-grain rice
3 tablespoons chopped fresh parsley

Heat the oil in a large skillet over low heat. Add the onion and cook until softened, about 8-10 minutes.

Add the ground pork. Raise the heat to medium-high and stir with a fork or wooden spoon to break up the lumps. When the meat has lost its pink, raw color, add the garlic and gizzards. Stir well. Cover the pan, lower the heat to medium, and cook 10 minutes, stirring occasionally.

Add the celery and bell pepper and cook 5 minutes more. Stir in the white pepper, cayenne, bay leaf, thyme, and salt. Add the chicken stock, stirring constantly to scrape up the cooking juices in the bottom of the skillet. Cook about 10 minutes more, stirring occasionally.

Add the chicken livers and cook 2 minutes, stirring (see above).

Stir in the rice. Reduce the heat to low, cover the pan, and cook until rice is tender, 15-20 minutes. Stir in the parsley before serving.

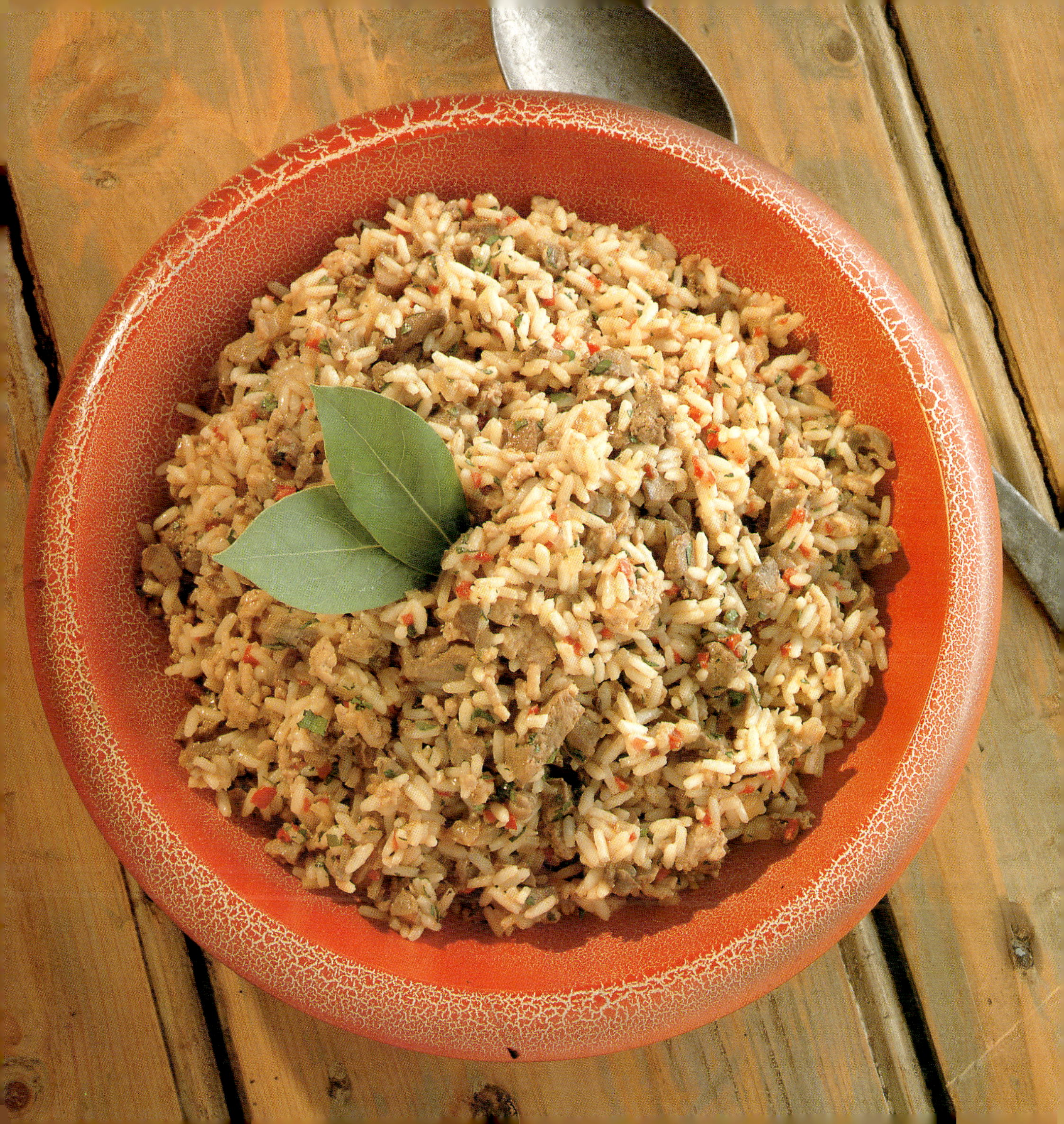

LIGHT SNACKS AND ACCOMPANIMENTS

SPOONBREAD

This light and fluffy bread is a close cousin to soufflé due to the beaten egg whites. Its texture gave rise to the name; it needs to be dished out with a spoon.

SERVES 4

2½ cups milk
1 cup yellow cornmeal
6 tablespoons butter or margarine
1 teaspoon salt
1½ teaspoons baking powder
3 eggs, separated

Preheat the oven to 375°F.

Heat the milk in a heavy saucepan. Just before it boils, beat in the cornmeal with a wire whisk. Cook over low heat about 10 minutes, stirring constantly.

Remove from the heat and beat in the butter or margarine, salt, and baking powder.

Add the egg yolks and beat until the mixture is smooth.

In a large bowl, beat the egg whites until they form stiff peaks. Fold them into the cornmeal mixture (see above right).

Pour into a well greased 6-cup baking dish (see note below). Bake until puffed and brown, 30-40 minutes. Serve with a spoon from the baking dish, and pass butter on the side.

COOK'S TIP

For soufflés a straight-sided soufflé dish is the key to success, though any tall, straight-sided oven proof baking dish will produce good results. Ensure that the dish is thoroughly buttered - especially around the rim to enable the soufflé mixture to slip easily up the sides.

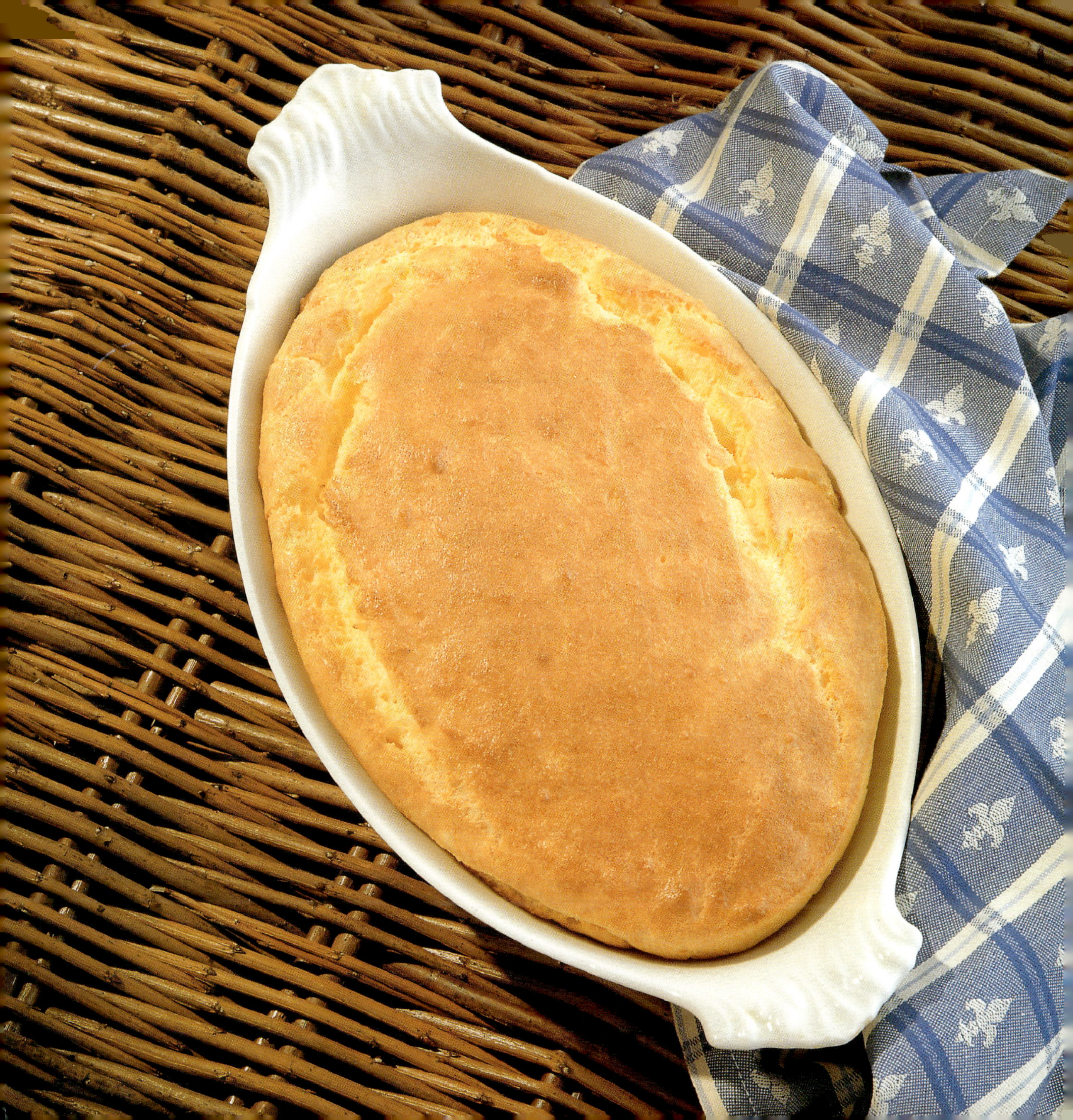

LIGHT SNACKS AND ACCOMPANIMENTS

Charleston Cheese Corn Bread

This tasty corn bread is a perfect side dish for a barbecue, but it is also delicious for a breakfast spread with butter and blackberry jam.

Serves 8

¾ cup yellow cornmeal

¾ cup flour

2 teaspoons baking powder

1 teaspoon salt

3 eggs

¾ cup buttermilk

¾ cup chopped corn kernels (fresh, frozen, or canned)

⅓ cup melted shortening or vegetable oil

1 cup shredded sharp cheddar cheese

2 tablespoons butter or margarine

Preheat the oven to 400°F.

In a large bowl, combine the cornmeal, flour, baking powder, and salt. Stir to mix.

In a medium-size bowl, beat the eggs until blended. Stir in the buttermilk, corn, shortening or oil, and ½ cup of the cheese.

Put the butter or margarine in an 8- or 9-inch skillet (with a heatproof handle) and place in the oven. Heat until melted. Remove from the oven and swirl the fat around to coat the bottom and sides of the skillet.

Add the liquid ingredients to the dry ones and mix until just blended. Pour the batter into the hot skillet and sprinkle with the remaining cheese.

Bake until the bread is golden brown and shrinks slightly from the edges of the skillet, 25-30 minutes. Cut into wedges and serve hot, with butter or margarine.

Hush Puppies

These deep-fried cornmeal nuggets are the essence of Southern cooking — to be eaten for breakfast, lunch and dinner and any time in between.

Serves 6

1 cup flour

2 teaspoons baking powder

1 teaspoon salt

1 cup cornmeal, preferably stone-ground

½ cup minced scallions

1 egg, beaten

1 cup buttermilk

oil for deep-frying

Sift the flour, baking powder, and salt into a medium-size bowl. Stir in the cornmeal and the scallions.

In a separate bowl, beat the egg and buttermilk together. Stir rapidly into the dry ingredients. Let the batter rest 20-30 minutes.

Heat oil in a deep-fryer or large, heavy saucepan to 375°F (to test the oil temperature, a bread cube dropped in the oil should brown in 40 seconds).

Drop the cornmeal mixture by tablespoonfuls into the hot oil. If the mixture seems too thick, add a little more buttermilk. Fry until golden brown. Drain on paper towels.

Serve the hush puppies while still hot.

DESSERTS

CORNMEAL BISCUITS

Another popular southern bread, these biscuits can be stuffed with slices of ham, cheddar cheese or just sweet butter.

MAKES ABOUT 12

1¼ cups flour
2½ teaspoons baking powder
¾ teaspoon salt
½ cup cornmeal, plus more for sprinkling
⅓ cup shortening or cold butter
¾ cup milk

Preheat the oven to 450°F.
Sift the flour, baking powder, and salt into a bowl. Stir in the cornmeal. Using a pastry blender or 2 knives scissor-fashion, cut the shortening or cold butter into the dry ingredients until the mixture is the consistency of coarse meal.

Make a well in the center and pour in the milk. Stir in quickly with a wooden spoon until the dough begins to pull away from the sides of the bowl, about 1 minute.

Turn the dough onto a lightly-floured surface and knead 8-10 times only (see above right). Roll out to a thickness of ½ inch. Cut into rounds with a floured 2-inch cookie cutter. Do not twist the cutter.

Sprinkle an ungreased cookie sheet lightly with cornmeal. Arrange the biscuits on the sheet, about 1 inch apart. Sprinkle the tops of the biscuits with more cornmeal.

Bake until golden brown, 10-12 minutes. Serve the biscuits hot, with butter or margarine.

VARIATION

For spicy cornmeal biscuits, stir ½ tablespoon of chopped jalapeño peppers into the mixture.

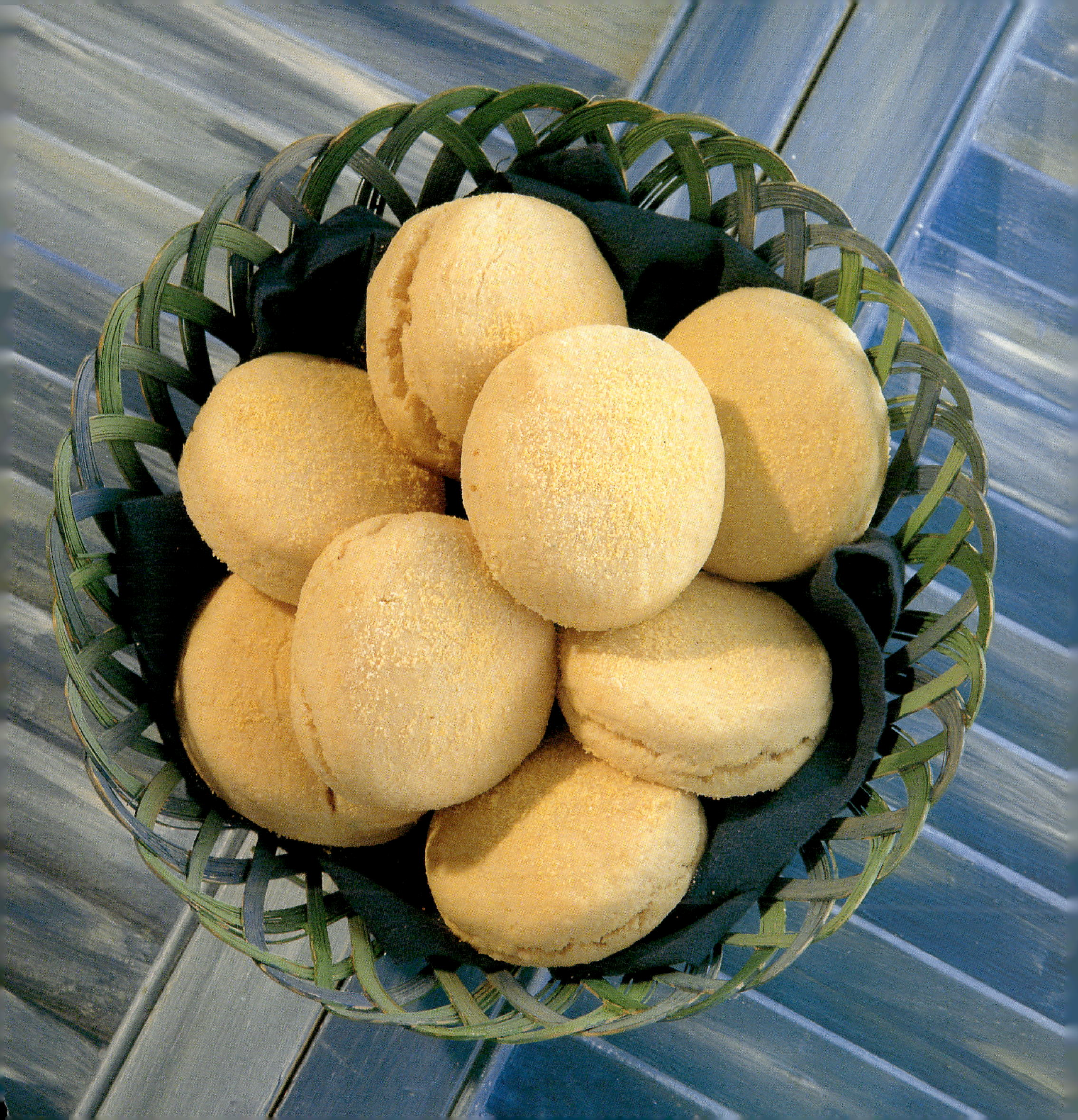

DESSERTS
FRENCH QUARTER BEIGNETS

IT IS A NEW ORLEANS TRADITION TO EAT THESE CRISPY, DECEPTIVELY LIGHT PASTRIES FOR BREAKFAST.

MAKES ABOUT 20

2 cups flour
1 teaspoon salt
1 tablespoon baking powder
1 teaspoon ground cinnamon
2 eggs
¼ cup granulated sugar
¾ cup milk
½ teaspoon vanilla extract
oil for deep-frying
confectioners' sugar, for sprinkling

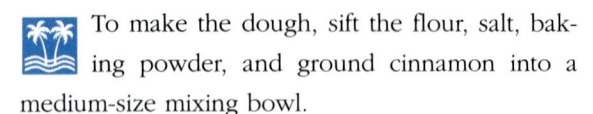

To make the dough, sift the flour, salt, baking powder, and ground cinnamon into a medium-size mixing bowl.

In a separate bowl, beat together the eggs, granulated sugar, milk, and vanilla. Pour the egg mixture into the dry ingredients and mix together quickly to form a dough.

Turn the dough onto a lightly-floured surface and knead thoroughly until smooth and elastic.

Heat oil in a deep-fryer or large, heavy saucepan to 375°F.

Roll out the dough to around ¼ inch thick. Slice diagonally into diamonds about 3 inches long.

Fry in the hot oil, turning once, until golden brown on both sides. Remove with tongs or a slotted spoon (see above) and drain well on paper towels. Sprinkle the beignets with confectioners' sugar before serving.

COOK'S TIP

ALTHOUGH DELICIOUS ON THEIR OWN, TRY SERVING THE BEIGNETS WITH A LAYER OF HONEY OR MAPLE SYRUP FOR A SPECIAL BREAKFAST TREAT.

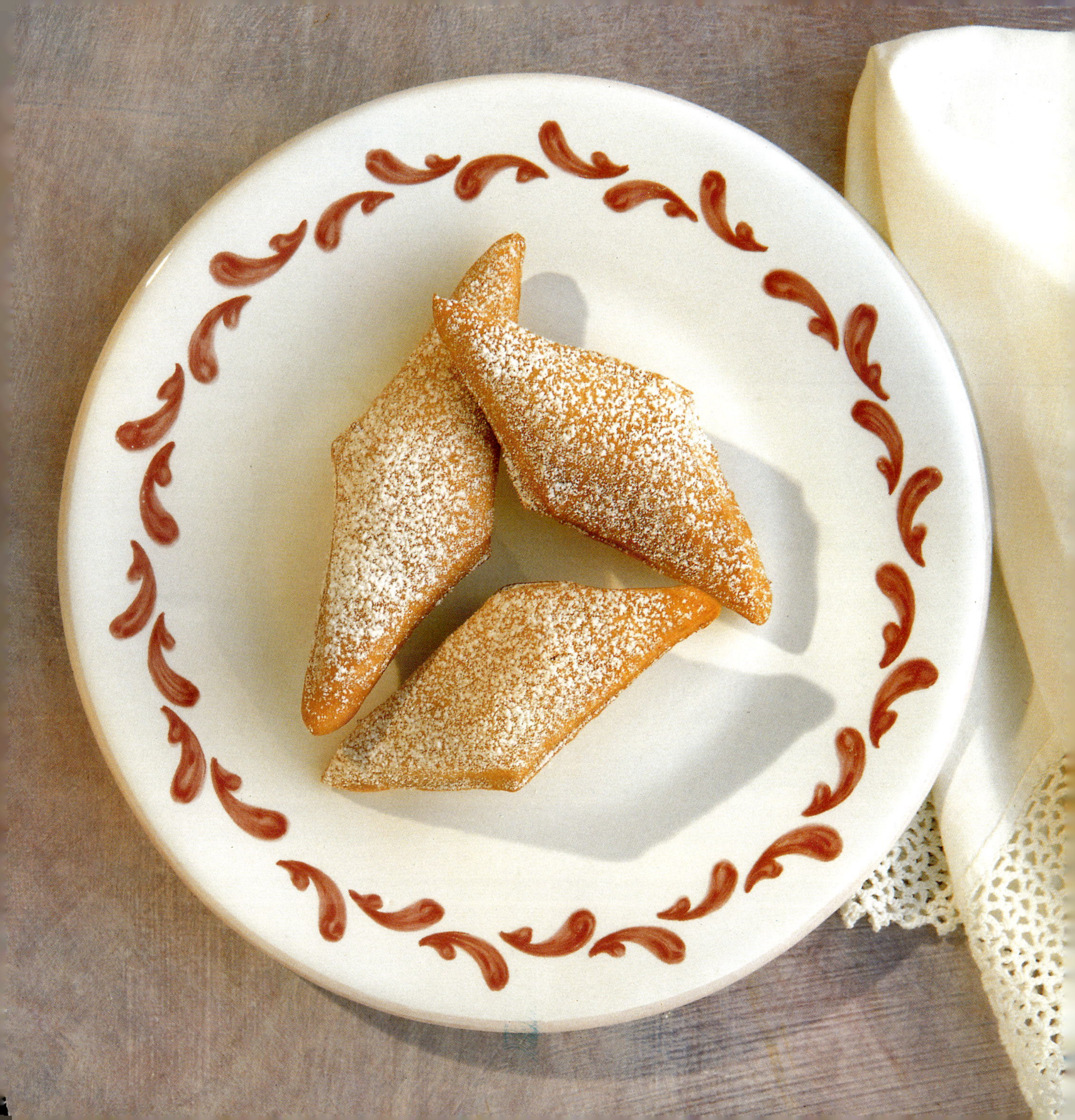

DESSERTS

GEORGIA PEANUT BUTTER PIE

Georgia is the patron state of the peanut and cooks there use it in all sorts of ingenious recipes. For true decadence serve this pie with a scoop of vanilla ice cream and a drizzle of hot fudge sauce.

SERVES 8

2 cups fine graham-cracker crumbs
¼ cup light brown sugar, firmly packed
6 tablespoons butter or margarine, melted
whipped cream or ice cream, for serving

FOR THE FILLING

3 egg yolks
½ cup granulated sugar
¼ cup light brown sugar, firmly packed
¼ cup cornstarch
⅛ teaspoon salt
2½ cups evaporated milk
2 tablespoons unsalted butter or margarine
1½ teaspoons vanilla extract
½ cup chunky peanut butter, preferably made from freshly-ground peanuts
¾ cup confectioners' sugar

Preheat the oven to 350°F.
Combine the crumbs, sugar, and butter or margarine in a bowl and blend well. Spread the mixture in a well-greased 9-inch pie pan, pressing evenly over the bottom and sides of the pan with your fingertips.
Bake the crumb crust 10 minutes. Remove from the oven and let cool. Leave the oven on.
Combine the egg yolks, granulated and brown sugars, cornstarch and salt in a heavy saucepan.
Slowly whisk in the milk. Cook over medium heat, stirring constantly, until the mixture thickens, about 8-10 minutes. Reduce the heat to very low and cook until very thick, 3-4 minutes more.
Beat in the butter or margarine. Stir in the vanilla. Remove from the heat. Cover the surface closely with plastic wrap and let cool.
In a small bowl combine the peanut butter with the confectioners' sugar, working with your fingers to blend the ingredients into small crumbs.
Sprinkle all but 3 tablespoons of the peanut butter crumbs over the bottom of the crumb crust.
Pour in the filling making an even layer. Sprinkle with the remaining crumbs. Bake 15 minutes.
Let the pie cool 1 hour. Serve with whipped cream or ice cream.

VARIATIONS

If preferred, use an equal amount of finely crushed vanilla wafers or ginger snaps in place of graham crackers for the crumb crust.

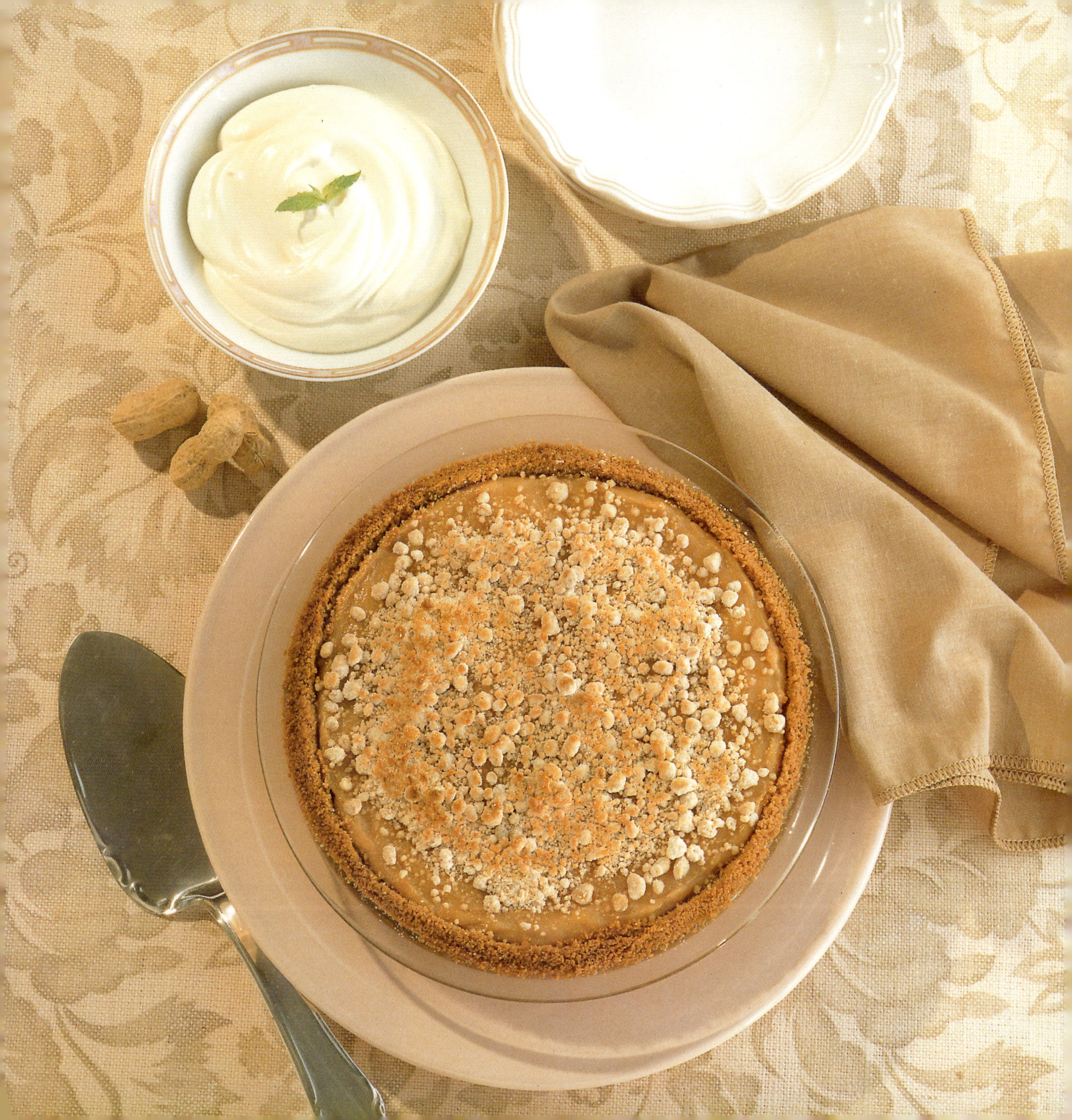

DESSERTS

MISSISSIPPI MUD CAKE

This sinfully rich cake is as black, rich and moist as the mud on the banks of the mighty Mississippi River, but it tastes a lot better!

SERVES 8-10

2 cups flour
⅛ teaspoon salt
1 teaspoon baking powder
1¼ cups strong brewed coffee
¼ cup bourbon or brandy
5 1-ounce squares unsweetened chocolate
1 cup (2 sticks) butter or margarine
2 cups sugar
2 eggs, at room temperature
1½ teaspoons vanilla extract
unsweetened cocoa powder
sweetened whipped cream or ice cream, for serving

Preheat the oven to 275°F.
Sift the flour, salt, and the baking powder together ensuring it is mixed in well.

Combine the coffee, bourbon or brandy, chocolate, and butter or margarine in the top of a double boiler. Heat until the chocolate and butter have melted, stirring occasionally.

Pour the chocolate mixture into a large bowl. Using an electric mixer on low speed, gradually beat in the sugar. Continue beating until the sugar has dissolved.

Raise the speed to medium and add the sifted dry ingredients. Mix well, then beat in the eggs and vanilla until thoroughly blended.

Pour the batter into a well-greased 3-quart bundt pan that has been dusted lightly with cocoa powder. Bake on a high shelf in the oven until a cake tester inserted in the cake comes out clean, about 1 hour 20 minutes.

Let cool in the pan for 15 minutes, then unmold onto a wire rack (see below). Let cool completely.

When the cake is cold, dust it lightly with cocoa powder. Serve with sweetened whipped cream or ice cream, if desired.

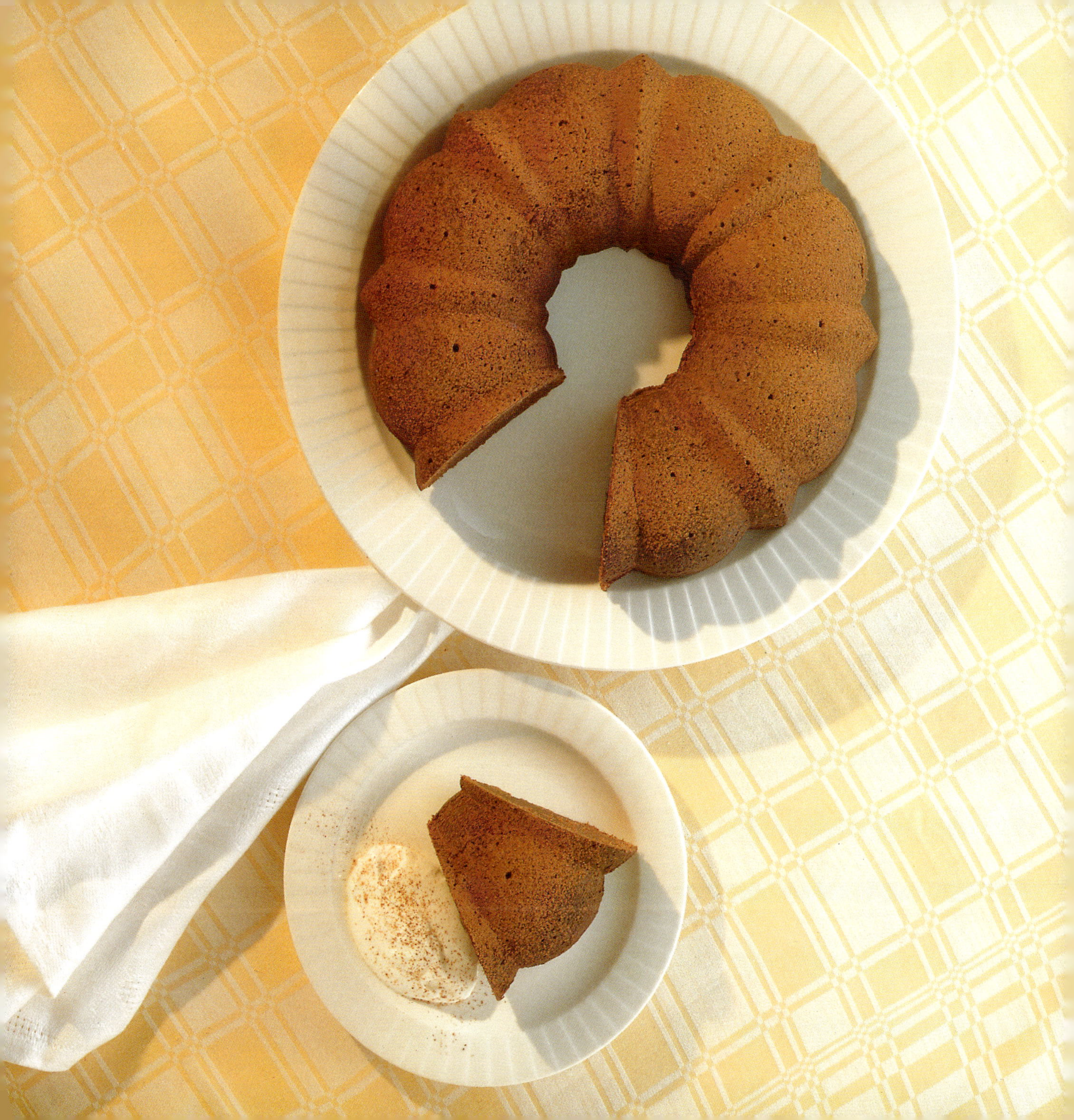

DESSERTS

BANANA LEMON LAYER CAKE

This light and airy layer cake is a birthday party classic. Serve it with a scoop of mango frozen yogurt for an exotic touch.

SERVES 8-10

2¼ cups cake flour
1¼ teaspoons baking powder
½ teaspoon salt
½ cup (1 stick) butter, at room temperature
1 cup granulated sugar
½ cup light brown sugar, firmly packed
2 eggs
½ teaspoon grated lemon rind
1 cup mashed very ripe bananas
1 teaspoon vanilla extract
¼ cup milk
¾ cup chopped walnuts

FOR THE FROSTING

½ cup (1 stick) butter, at room temperature
4½ cups confectioners' sugar
¾ teaspoon grated lemon rind
3-5 tablespoons fresh lemon juice

Preheat the oven to 350°F. Grease 2 9-inch round cake pans, and line the bottom of each with a disk of wax paper that has been greased with a little butter.

Sift the flour with the baking powder and salt.

In a large mixing bowl, cream the butter with the sugars until light and fluffy. Beat in the eggs, one at a time. Stir in the lemon rind.

In a small bowl mix the mashed bananas with the vanilla and milk. Add the banana mixture and the dry ingredients to the butter mixture alternately in 2 or 3 batches and stir until just blended. Fold in the nuts.

Divide the batter between the cake pans and spread it out evenly. Bake until a cake tester inserted in the center comes out clean, 30-35 minutes. Let stand 5 minutes before unmolding onto a wire rack. Peel off the wax paper.

For the frosting, cream the butter until smooth, then gradually beat in the sugar. Stir in the lemon rind and enough juice to make the frosting a spreadable consistency.

Set one of the cake layers on a serving plate. Cover with about one-third of the frosting. Top with the second cake layer. Spread the remaining frosting evenly over the top and sides of the cake.

Decorate with tiny slivers of lemon rind.

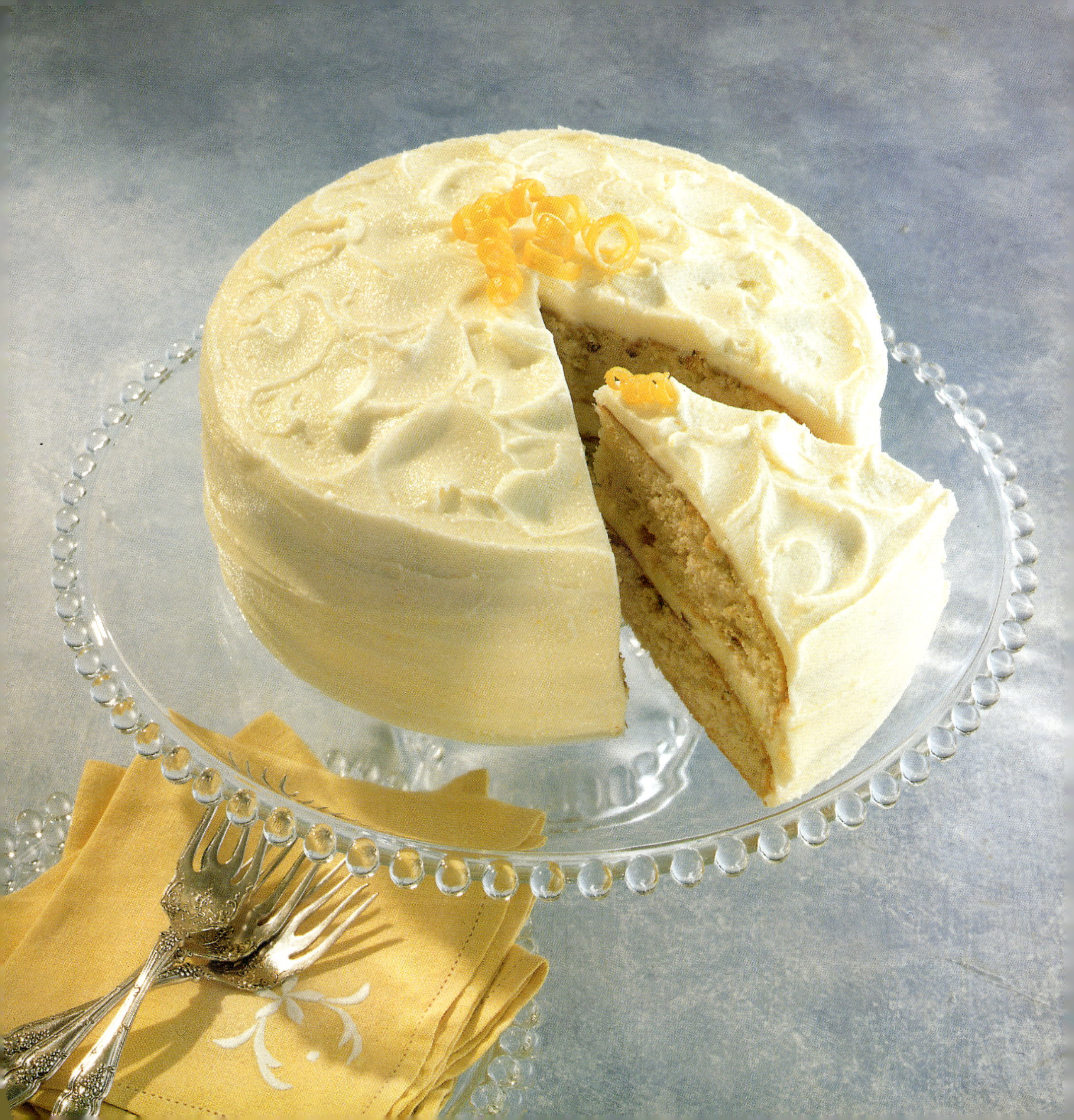

DESSERTS

PINK GRAPEFRUIT SHERBET

On a sultry summer night there is no better dessert than this tart, delicate sherbet. If you're having a gala dinner it is an ideal palate freshener between courses.

SERVES 8

¾ cup granulated sugar
½ cup water
4 cups strained freshly-squeezed pink grapefruit juice
1-2 tablespoons fresh lemon juice
confectioners' sugar, to taste

In a small heavy saucepan, dissolve the granulated sugar in the water over medium heat, without stirring. When the sugar has dissolved, boil 3-4 minutes. Remove from the heat and let cool.

Pour the cooled sugar syrup into the grapefruit juice (see right). Stir well. Taste the mixture and adjust the flavor by adding some lemon juice or a little confectioners' sugar, if necessary, but do not over-sweeten.

Pour the mixture into a metal or plastic freezer container and freeze until softly set, about 3 hours.

Remove from the container and chop roughly into 3-inch pieces. Place in a food processor or blender and process until smooth. Return the mixture to the freezer container and freeze again until set. Repeat this freezing and chopping process 2 or 3 times, until a smooth consistency is obtained.

Alternatively, freeze the sherbet in an ice cream maker, following the manufacturer's instructions.

VARIATION

For Orange Sherbet, substitute an equal amount of orange juice for the grapefruit juice and increase the lemon juice to 3-4 tablespoons, or to taste. For additional flavor, add 1 tablespoon finely grated orange rind. If blood oranges are available, their deep red color gives a dramatic effect, and the flavor is exciting as well.

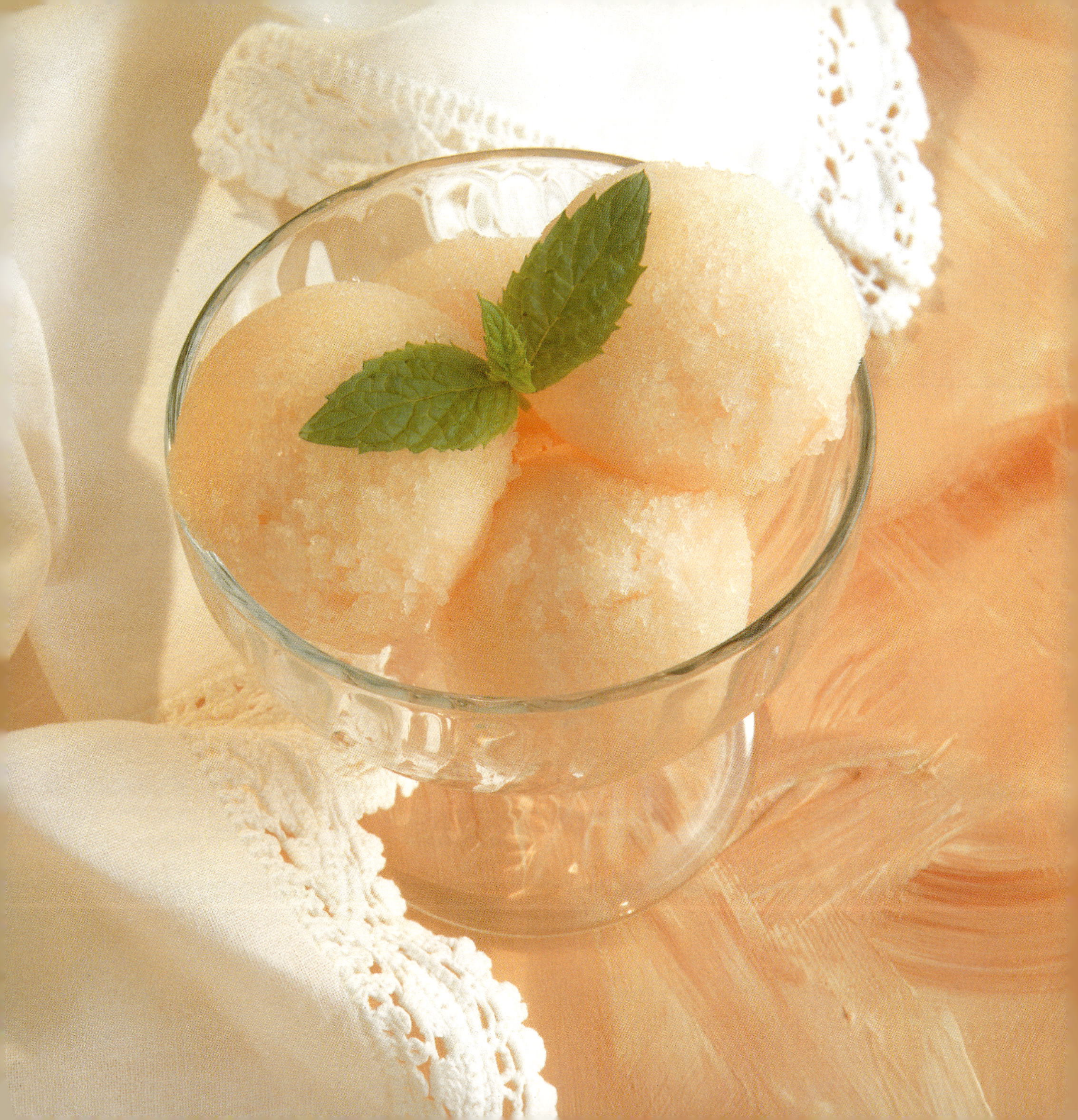

DESSERTS

KEY LIME SHERBET

If you can't find fresh key limes or bottled key lime juice, use regular limes. The taste will still evoke the turquoise waters, palm trees and sugar sand beaches of the Florida Keys.

SERVES 4

1¼ cups granulated sugar
2½ cups water
grated rind of 1 lime
¾ cup freshly-squeezed key lime juice
1-2 tablespoons fresh lemon juice
confectioners' sugar, to taste

In a small heavy saucepan, dissolve the granulated sugar in the water, without stirring, over medium heat. When the sugar has dissolved, boil 5-6 minutes. Remove from the heat and let cool.

Combine the cooled sugar syrup and lime rind and juice in a measure or bowl (see right). Stir well. Taste and adjust the flavor by adding lemon juice or some confectioners' sugar, if necessary. Take care not to oversweeten.

Freeze the mixture in an ice cream maker, following the manufacturer's instructions.

If you do not have an ice cream maker, pour the mixture into a metal or plastic freezer container and freeze until softly set, about 3 hours.

Remove from the container and chop roughly into 3-inch pieces. Place in a food processor or blender and process until smooth. Return the mixture to the freezer container and freeze again until set. Repeat this freezing and chopping process 2 or 3 times, until a smooth consistency is obtained.

COOK'S TIP

IF USING AN ICE CREAM MAKER FOR THESE SHERBETS, CHECK THE MANUFACTURER'S INSTRUCTIONS TO FIND OUT THE FREEZING CAPACITY. IF NECESSARY, HALVE THE RECIPE QUANTITIES.

INDEX

Avocado
   Miami chilled soup 8
   and papaya salad 12

Banana Lemon Layer Cake 58
Beignets, French Quarter 52
Blackened Chicken Breasts 40

Cajun 'Popcorn' with Basil
   Mayonnaise 20
Catfish, fried 28
Charleston Cheese Corn Bread
   48
Chicken
   blackened, 40
   oven fried 38
   Collards and Rice 42
Corn Maque Choux 42
Cornmeal Biscuits 50
Crab Bayou 18
Crawfish or Shrimp Etouffée 22

Dirty Rice 44

Eggplant, shrimp-stuffed 26

French Quarter Beignets 52
Fried Catfish Fillets with
   Piquant Sauce 28
Fromajardis 16

Georgia Peanut Butter Pie 54

Hush Puppies 48

Jambalaya, Pork 34

Key Lime Sherbet 62

Miami Chilled Avocado Soup 8
Mississippi Mud Cake 56

Oven Fried Chicken 31

Palm Beach Papaya and
   Avocado Salad 12
Peas, black-eyed warm salad 14
Pecan Stuffed Pork Chops 36
Pink Grapefruit Sherbet 60
Pork Jambalaya 34
Pork Chops, pecan stuffed 36

Rabbit, smothered 32

Seafood and Sausage Gumbo 30
Shrimp
   and corn bisque 10
   Creole 24
   etouffée 22
   stuffed eggplant 26
Smothered Rabbit 32
Spoonbread 46

Warm Salad of Black-Eyed Peas
   14

64